Let Me Explain

Let Me Explain

Poems

Gaylord Brewer

Iris Press
Oak Ridge, Tennessee

Copyright © 2006 by Gaylord Brewer

All rights reserved. No portion of this book may be reproduced in any form or by any means, including electronic storage and retrieval systems, without explicit, prior written permission of the publisher, except for brief passages excerpted for review and critical purposes.

Iris Press is an imprint of
The Iris Publishing Group, Inc

www.irisbooks.com

Library of Congress Cataloging-in-Publication Data

Brewer, Gaylord, 1965-
 Let me explain : poems / Gaylord Brewer.
    p. cm.
 ISBN-13: 978-0-916078-67-6 (hardcover : alk. paper)
 ISBN-10: 0-916078-67-1 (hardcover : alk. paper)
 ISBN-13: 978-0-916078-68-3 (pbk. : alk. paper)
 ISBN-10: 0-916078-68-x (pbk. : alk. paper)
 I. Title.
 PR3552.R4174L48 2006
 811'.54—dc22
                                    2006002406

Acknowledgments

Thanks to the editors of the publications where these poems appeared, at times in slightly different forms and titles:

Alimentum: "Apologia for a Frozen Surplus," "Apologia for Cooking"
American Poetry Journal: "Apologia for an Autumnal Moment"
Asheville Poetry Review: "Apologia to Every Woman I Ever Wanted," "Apologia to the Son of a Bitch who Stole My Sandals on the Beach"
Bayou: "Apologia to My Publisher for Replacing the Author Photo"
Birmingham Poetry Review: "Apologia for the First Day of School"
Black Zinnias: "Apologia to War Emblem, 'Dud as a Stud'"
Blue Mesa Review: "Apologia for My Morning at the Milton Conference," "Apologia for Private Drinking," "Apologia for Public Drinking"
Briar Cliff Review: "Apologia for 'The Yolk of Marriage'"
Center: "Apologia for the First Day of School"
Cimarron Review: "Apologia for Separateness"
Dos Passos Review: "Apologia for a Simple Restorative"
88: "Apologia for America at War"
Fire (UK): "Apologia to Morning Fog," "Apologia to the Red Planet," "Apologia to the South of France for Nicaragua"
Greensboro Review: "Apologia for Stigmata"
Gulf Coast: "Apologia to the Trout at Meadow Farm"
Hurricane Review: "Apologia for Rain," "Apologia for the Storm as It Arrives to Us," "Apologia to War Emblem, 'Dud as a Stud'"
Iron Horse Literary Review: "Apologia for Postcards," "Apologia to a Woman's Ear"
Linq (Australia): "Apologia for Birding," "Apologia for the Bone Box," "Apologia for Waking in Hell"

Margie: "Apologia for Epigraphs"
North American Review: "Apologia to Anne Sexton"
Paper Street: "Apologia to Renaldo, and Goodbye"
Plainsongs (editor's best-of-issue): "Apologia for Full Manly Vigor"
Poetry East: "Apologia for a Thanksgiving Pissed Away"
Poetry International: "Apologia for My Dog's Happiness, with a Motif of Chekhov"
Portland Review: "Apologia for Charley"
Red Wheelbarrow: "Apologia to a Papaya for the Ode I Promised"
Rive Gauche: "Apologia for the Indifference of Animals"
River Oak Review: "Apologia for a Martini in Winter," "Apologia for the Martini Glass," "Apologia for Wordiness"
River Styx: "Apologia for My Father the Killer"
Santa Clara Review: "Apologia for the Concerns of Literature," "Apologia of the Traveler"
Seam (U.K.): "Apologia for the Last Family Vacation," "Apologia for My Addiction to the Thursday Horoscope," "Apologia to a Billowing Curtain"
Slant: "Apologia for the Storm as It Arrives to Us"
Smartish Pace: "Apologia for an Uninvited Disciple," "Apologia for Ten Days of Happiness"
South Carolina Review: "Apologia for Cash and Luck," "Apologia, Rescinded, to the Month Ahead"
Southeast Review: "Apologia for a Modest Skull Collection"
Southern Poetry Review: "Apologia to the Victims of the Storm"
Spindrift: "Apologia to the Moment Before My Death"
Tulane Review: "Apologia for the Fish I Overcooked on Good Friday"
Two Rivers Review: "Apologia for a September Garden"
West Branch: "Apologia to the Poem for Grace's Estate Auction, Interrupted by a Dog"

"Apologia for the Last Word" appeared in the anthology *Red, White, and Blues: Poets on the Promise of America* (Iowa City: Iowa UP, 2004).

Author's Note

The first of these poems were written in September 2002 in Lascassas, Tennessee (pop. 120). My wife was in Texas and the dog and I ran the property. The manuscript was mostly completed—with the exception of six or eight pieces added late—by December 2003 in the same, albeit noisier, room. In the interim, I had a productive stay at the Julia and David White Artists' Colony, Costa Rica, during the summer of 2003.

For years, I'd been periodically experimenting with (and rejecting) ideas for an extended sequence of connected poems, a form with the elasticity to accommodate a variety of tones and subjects. Apparently, something about the apologias—and their challenges and opportunities vis-à-vis my usual fetishes—felt right. For more than two years I wrote nothing else.

Too much of a good thing, Mae West encouraged us, is wonderful. We'll see.

In memoriam:
Bill White,
a good and kind man.

When the right virtuous Edward Wotton and I were at the Emperor's Court together, we gave ourselves to learn horsemanship of John Pietro Pugliano, one that with great commendation had the place of an esquire in his stable. And he, according to the fertileness of the Italian wit, did not only afford us the demonstration of his practice, but sought to enrich our minds with the contemplations therein, which he thought most precious. But with none I remember mine ears were at any time more loaden, than when (either angered with slow payment, or moved with our learner-like admiration) he exercised his speech in the praise of his faculty.

—Sir Philip Sidney, *An Apology for Poetry*

Contents

Apologia for a Modest Skull Collection • 17

I

Apologia, Rescinded, to the Month Ahead • 21
Apologia to a Billowing Curtain • 22
Apologia to a Papaya for the Ode I promised • 24
Apologia for an Uninvited Disciple • 26
Apologia for Pablo Neruda's 99th Birthday • 28
Apologia for Wordiness • 30
Apologia for Birding • 31
Apologia for Ten Days of Happiness • 32
Apologia for Your Death • 33
Apologia for Our Last Family Vacation • 34
Apologia to the Poem about Grace's Estate Auction, Interrupted by a Dog • 35
Apologia for Epigraphs • 37
Apologia to Every Woman I Ever Wanted • 38
Apologia to a Woman's Ear • 39
Apologia for Cash and Luck • 40
Apologia to the South of France for Nicaragua • 41
Apologia to the Son of a Bitch who Stole My Sandals on the Beach • 43
Apologia for Postcards • 44

II

Apologia for My Father the Killer • 47
Apologia to War Emblem, "Dud as a Stud" • 48

Apologia to Alan Dugan and Bill Shoemaker • 49
Apologia for Missing Cousin Willie's Burial • 50
Apologia for T., Five Years Gone • 51
Apologia of the Traveler • 52
Apologia to My Publisher for Replacing the Author Photo • 53
Apologia for My Addiction to the Thursday Horoscope • 54
Apologia for the First Day of School • 55
Apologia for Stigmata • 56
Apologia for "The Yolk of Marriage" • 57
Apologia for My Morning at the Milton Conference • 58
Apologia for Charley • 59
Apologia to Gregory Hemingway • 60
Apologia for the Concerns of Literature • 61
Apologia for America at War • 62
Apologia for Voting • 63
Apologia for the Storm as It Arrives to Us • 64
Apologia for an Autumnal Moment • 65
Apologia for a Common Sabbath • 66
Apologia to Anne Sexton • 67
Apologia for Waking in Hell • 68
Apologia to the Moment before My Death • 69
Apologia to Renaldo, and Goodbye • 70
Apologia for the Highway Dead • 71
Apologia to the Last Full Moon of the Year • 72
Apologia for the Bone Box • 73
Apologia for the Last Word • 74

III

Apologia for the Indifference of Animals • 77
Apologia for a September Garden • 78
Apologia for a Bat • 79
Apologia for Separateness • 80
Apologia for the Fish I Overcooked on Good Friday • 81
Apologia to the Trout at Meadow Farm • 82
Apologia to the First Snake of the Year • 83
Apologia to the Victims of the Storm • 84

Apologia to the First Full Moon of Spring • 85
Apologia for a Simple Restorative • 86
Apologia for Rain • 87
Apologia for the Martini Glass • 88
Apologia for a Martini in Winter • 89
Apologia for a Frozen Surplus • 90
Apologia for Cooking • 91
Apologia for a Thanksgiving Pissed Away • 93
Apologia for a Shopping List • 94
Apologia for Tuesday Bachelor Dinners • 95
Apologia for Private Drinking • 96
Apologia for Public Drinking • 97
Apologia for Full Manly Vigor • 98
Apologia for Erotic Photography and a Woman Bathing • 99
Apologia for My Wife's Sleeplessness • 100
Apologia to the Red Planet • 101
Apologia for Morning Fog • 102
Apologia for My Dog's Happiness, with a Motif of Chekhov • 103
Apologia on the Eve of Jasper's 12th Birthday • 104

Apologia for a Modest Skull Collection

Invariably they enter, at last, my library—
crucible, lab, chamber; war room, sanctum, nest—
as do these two, trail eyes along impeccably
even volumes, world knick knacks, quirky detritus.
Gangly spectacled man and plump new wife,
and I can't decide if they have crashed the party
of my privacy or if I have ushered them
to its sticky thread. I divine their cautious steps
as reverential, but, again, it's a busy room.
My rows of jawbones and unknowable shards,
my odd teeth and fragments. I move them along
to intact, albeit decayed, varieties of the family
Canidae. Wizard at his cabala, alchemist stamping
fiery metals, maestro erect on the podium,
I move them along to my showpieces: illicit flamingo
cradled in tissue from Lake Nakuru, Kenya;
little buck-toothed gopher bartered at sunset
from a Santo Domingo Indian in a New Mexico field;
large-socketed rabbit, rescued roadside
in mangle of fur, then bleached to pure,
infinite white; and lastly, most exquisitely,
my mockingbird, cartilage of beak still thrusting
its point as if modeling some tiny masquerade.
This I even perch judiciously in my palm for the pair
to circle, peer into, and *ahh*. But not to touch.

I

When he got back the envelope was gone together with the spanish letter but he had the english letter and it was separated into three parts along the lines of its folding and it was dogeared and coffeestained and stained with other stains some of which may have been blood. He'd been in jail once in Kentucky, once in Tennessee, and three times in Texas. When he pulled into the yard he got out and walked stiffly to the house and knocked at the kitchen door.

•

You have the opportunity to tell the truth here. Here. In three days you will go to Saltillo and then you will no have this opportunity. It will be gone. Then the truth will be in other hands. You see. We can make the truth here. Or we can lose it. But when you leave here it will be too late.

•

I am the one when I go someplace then there is no laughing. When I go there then they stop laughing.

—Cormac McCarthy

Apologia, Rescinded, to the Month Ahead

—day one, noon, Ciudad Colón, Costa Rica

Your boulder presses me close, your stone
of weeks, gravel days, sand of an hour, grit
of each minute and the implacable dust of seconds.
Already I sweat from your humid exhortations.
I too smell resignation fronting the clouds
that shoulder afternoon across our mountain,
resignation and danger, dark necessities.
This morning I defeated the scorpion in the shower.
A white-haired man who bargained coffee plants
had five grown daughters, eyes so blue they glowed.
See where we've arrived? Pay attention—
there is a shade of laughter beneath your doubt.
Or perhaps, rather, you are a sack, lip curled,
to fill as one desires with bird call, steaming flowers,
a sea wind. Perhaps with sweet papaya
longer than American footballs and a sticky bulge
of mangos, each the size of a child's head.
Perhaps I have places in my life, Month, people
and animals, times deserving explanation,
a frank account of whereabouts. Certainly
I offer you nothing, nada, before they're satisfied.

Apologia to a Billowing Curtain

Our squabble blew in last night, late,
when you took exception to hot snores
and whipped my erect flashlight
into crashing darkness. I closed the fins
of window and checked my equipment—
still potent, explosive, blinding.
Come dawn, rooms needed breath.
I've learned morning's when I want you most,
your pliant eastern position. But the cost!
Bitter over coffee, I eye blowsy maneuvers,
lunges, quips, typical unpredictability.
With a disregard for my privacy
you've slowly taught me to admire,
you flick my shopping list to the floor,
send my secret area codes flying.
Your stiff fabric brushes covers
of two broken dictionaries—
one idiomatic, another etymological.
Your language, all shape and shift,
turbulent show, rustles silent fury
without reason. A puff enough to provoke
as raucous world wakes in you again.
Your pair of sunflowers expand and contract,
bend and beckon, tease toward the couch
then withdraw suddenly back flat
against oscillations of shadow and light.
You're a flirt, but I'm easy with the dance.
Though I'd prefer, speaking freely,
that each time in and out you might resist
flipping with bosomy exasperation
the first page of a manuscript of poems,
caring only, it seems, for title and dedication,
alternately arousing and dismissing my sheets

in your airy, spooky embrace of tent,
shroud, sail, your aggressive cotton robe
for around the house and in front of me.

Apologia to a Papaya for the Ode I Promised

As I cradled you safely from market,
proud of your length and heft,
your belly fatter than a circle of hands,
as I marveled at your sad, exotic skin
of mottled yellow, I knew without knowing
that an ode was owed. But as one day passed,
then another, this adoption enlarged
to a burden I somehow couldn't equal.
I would open the hamper to feel you—
cold now—to turn you, stare dumbly down.
Then this morning, after last night's storm,
I shuffled groggy and dispirited to the kitchen.
You loomed there—mammoth, monolithic,
undaunted where I had displayed you
to dinner guests, who stared from behind
their drinks and would not touch you,
wouldn't take you away as midnight prize.
Shakier than a man my age should be,
I cleared plates, rinsed my longest blade,
balanced you gently on your rump.
Strips of skin thudded like wet bark to the table.
Your heavy flesh, darker than any carrot,
glistened nearly red. I sculpted an edible form,
reduced it to squares, began to stack them.
Then, your ripe secret opened, caviar of seed.
I stacked more carcass; the pile grew.
Suddenly I understood—oppression continuing
in same degree, merely shape redefined.
On impulse, I skewed a square and ate.
I chewed, swallowed. I lifted a second slab,
slippery between fingers, and ate again.
Here's the last surprise—I didn't like the taste.
So I stood there, trying to think it through.

Then, hands working on their own, into the sack
you went, your guts and seed, story
and violation, my failure, all into the bin.

Apologia for an Uninvited Disciple

> each day
> a succession of flowers or blood
> —Neruda

Or otherwise in English—apostle, student,
protégé, minnow, mollusk, sapling, mud.
But he approached as a man, clay man
with clay man's beard, but anyway not a boy.
Perhaps arrived salty from port Valparaíso,
perhaps sprung stinking from forest compost.
I don't know. I was just awake—day yawning
and uncertain—when I saw him pass
my curtain. Averted eyes and quick step,
nonchalant shoulders—second pass, a third.
What could I do but invite the poor beast in,
offer a chair where my privacy had loafed?
He feigned surprise, refused, sat. I demonstrated
the nave of lemon, butter of artichoke,
torrent of tomato. He nodded behind
his blindfold, smacked lips happily confused.
I began again, slowly, in compact phrases—
briny merchandise of sea, winter flowers torn
to ash, sandy necktie of country where
I once knocked sadly on every door searching
for myself. Of men called Federico, Cesár,
brothers I'd never met, all dead and waiting.
Recalled the healing bridge of women's thighs
and the radiant black ruby at its source,
a bird alone and silenced in storm.
He is, I believe, a slow man from a slow family.
When quizzed, he steps to shore to study
foamy text, strains toward archival notes
dropped from bells in their bronze bindings.
His translations gibberish, but faithful.

He pantomimes dreams of regret and self-disgust.
I offer orange, knife, a frowning reed hat.
He tends plants willingly, but I entreat him
not to blind himself when he closes his eyes.
If he's to carry my mark when I banish him,
he must dress murder in his heart, open my throat
in a tender stroke before kissing goodbye
and spitting at my shoes. If he's one of mine,
I need him dangerous when he paddles away
from this island in flames. The answer to the exam,
no one can teach—he is obliged to be happy.

Apologia for Pablo Neruda's 99th Birthday

> take your bread and your apple,
> your heart and your horse
> and mount guard on the frontier

Arenal appeared to us, for us
her cloud rose—
a moment only
those peaks, blue and ragged,
dominated opaque heaven.
Smoke insinuating
her hot mouth.
We raised a toast to you,
father, brother, cousin, *hauso,* priest,
hands holding
cool *guaro,* glasses nodding,
touching, speaking.
At midnight we bathed in her
thermal waters,
night jungle
and sonorous, aggressive life-chant,
choked vines, mossy invitations,
parasitic blooms.
Tendril of heat above the surface—
here is where her burning,
iron-stained spring
ripples entry.
Always the dark canopy
of your historical song,
America's awful splendor, disregarded
path of blood.
Epiphytes profit without harm,
benefit the host.
So we evolve together.

Our slick, steaming bodies
splashed on regenerative stones,
pale fish dripping,
friend, laughing,
surging in your memory.

—for Virgil Suárez

Apologia for Wordiness

Today is Sunday, day of unspoken matter,
no unheeded gesture, no casual charm.
A flycatcher rides the bend of pine,
a rufous hummingbird stiffly below
with its emerald back to me. These names
may be invoked without hesitation. One,
breast yellow, dips away keening. The other,
tiny, intense, holds against sway, looks
left, holds. I step as close as foliage allows.
In a moment, though I do not know it yet,
I will photograph a young woman
shooing two Labradors from her landing.
Later, I'm confident, I will climb to the grove.
Manzanas de agua, color of red polish,
are rumored ripe and dropping
from limbs. I have no reason to disbelieve.
Possibly I will fill a canvas bag with these,
with small tart limes that litter the hill.
The hummer hangs above me, goes in a blur.
Wand of limb remains; I watch it move.
Bamboo fifty feet above creaks like steel beams
in argument of air. Labrador, bamboo,
manzana de agua—see? No regret, no loss.
Twice, I've forgotten to silence the ringer
on the telephone. The mountain shifts,
disperses, blue and sure. Today is Sunday.
Of course I lied. The poem's title is, always,
"Apologia for Not Missing You Enough."

Apologia for Birding

> And to you, Miss O'Shaughnessy, adieu. I leave you
> the rara avis on the table as a little momento.
> —Caspar Gutman, *The Maltese Falcon*

We include this epigraph as modest buffer
of "cool" against our hero's humbling epiphany—
he's a bird geek. Look at him, dripping between
banana trees, mashing trails of gooey mango
where butterflies dance drunk when sky's clear.
Right now it's pouring. How did this happen?
There he perches, drenched, absurd in the terrain,
taking a muddied hill through steamed lenses
of field glasses. Focus? Where a squirrel cuckoo
just disappeared into thick second-growth.
The bird's no fool; it's raining. Look at this clown,
wanting to glimpse the last wildness—why,
he can't even bring himself to use "I" in such a big,
slippery landscape. 3000 feet. You'd think
he'd unearthed his own Macchu Picchu up here.
Look at him grinning, at the belly of strange apples
in knapsack. Where is everybody, anyway?
Dry in their rooms, bud, with book and mug.
In cuckoo land, rain thins. The bird looses
a sharp *kip! wheeu!* and hops into sight. It preens
wings back to their rufous luster, long white-tipped
rectrices to full and airy distinction. It leaps
to descending glide and goofy man pursues,
lurching in sludge and rot and heavy tropical grass.
What beauty! 20 inches if one. *God—the nest!*
Now this is a language a geek can live with.

Apologia for Ten Days of Happiness

They were pure hell, cousin. The smiles
and handshakes, fruit picked sweet from the tree,
sunny mornings and cool, dripping afternoons.
Long evening meals and conversations,
languorous yawning time, the books, the sightings.
Hell, hell, hell. I closed those windows—
stifled rooms with reassuring gloom.
Started wearing the same damp shirts, stained shorts,
eating nothing but cold rice. My feet black.
Of course, I play hit the bottle, faithful friend
who never gave up on me, even at my cheeriest—
gin, rum, whiskey, whatever I can get, and not
for what they'd call pleasure, cousin.
To slay that goofy grinning bastard
and his satisfied sleep. When they knock now,
nosing in for more good times, I answer with a snarl,
fistfuls of oozy sweat, cracked door, a squint.
Sorry, no comprende. Allow them a glimpse
of the real thing, old style, endangered and dangerous
and right next door. Lordly beast, ascendant,
belly stuffed, picking teeth with a bone
that might look terribly familiar. My smile now one
I know and love, that has saved my life again.

Apologia for Your Death

"Nobody has it easy"—your mantra swirled
in smoke above crossed ankles, repeated
to a choir of ice rattling a glass over sunset,
ice a private glacier of complacent fury,
ice the crystalline die of careful good fortune,
ice of diamond skulls cut for posterity.
Nobody has it easy, and too often these days
that choice bit of fat is a hard swallow
even holy rivers of wine can't clear, even
celebration dissolve. You fine, generous man,
you man apart. Too often these not-easy days,
the tickle of sweat seems no fun at all,
unnatural, unattractive, uninviting, sprung
from some greasy excess; black handkerchief
across brow just doesn't turn the trick.
Nobody has it easy. Nobody wins, nobody stays.
You're a good ole boy, with cash to burn.
And sooner you're gone, wheezy benevolence,
manufactured despair, flatulence delivered
for a world's salvation, hymns of poolside
condolence, sooner suffering, amen, is through
and your bones ground to shit, the better.

Apologia for Our Last Family Vacation

> Left eye, right eye, take a look around,
> everybody's heading for a hole in the ground.
> —Warren Zevon

Like Clearwater, before "undesirables" ruined it.
Dad proud with his case of scripture, skinny legs.
Mom messaging lotion across her scars.
Little sis with her secret bottles and boyfriend.
Sun's up every day, whatever day is; all night too.
And it is hot. It is hot, it is hot, it is a sauna,
it is a radiator, it is matchstick to a tropical keg.
It is one hot bastard. We limp the beach, feet raw
in coals of sand. We squint where black sea boils,
where fin-less sharks churn for Chinese blood.
Alligators swim upside down, happy and hungry,
white bellies blinding. We pick rotted, spiky fruit
and gag on it. Wipe chins with torn fingers.
Toss pulp to distract beaks from eyes, ears, privates.
Up the boardwalk, boyfriend cruises in, top down,
same damned blue orbs, red skin, horny smile.
Piled in back, the chains and whips of afternoon
aerobics. Sis crawls to the shower to purge, rinse,
gargle with the vodka beneath the drain.
Mom and dad share a cigarette and stare out
from the deck of a flaming bungalow, time-share,
dream realized, ours for the next ten thousand years.

Apologia to the Poem about Grace's Estate Auction, Interrupted by a Dog

To begin seriously, a study of memory and mixed feelings.
Begin, even, in France, and not just France but perfumed
and sunny southern France, where I lived in a stone cabin
built on a path, so when I opened doors at either end
local mutts stormed the house, yelping, chasing,
raising dust. This the sort of drama I intended, landscapes,
rending juxtapositions. See, that's when Grace died at last,
that summer. I missed the funeral, recalled instead,
from a sleepy terrace above the valley, sipping chilled rosé,
the last time I visited her tiny box of a home,
mottled fingers probing my face. This the set-up later
events deserved, returning to that house, hollow rooms,
backyard jumble of chairs, dolls, lamps, gawkers, numbered
junk—unlit candles, doilies, cheap gifts I recognized.
An auctioneer's booming voice and humor. See the potential,
the pathos, metaphor for fragile and fleeting lives,
dreams, conceits, accumulations? All of us in the boat.
The poignant possibilities. Unfortunately, this poem was
wrecked by an old black Labrador, Fudge, christened Negrito
by us artists. As I began to quiet myself, receive morning
in a reflective, humble mood, I heard his wheezing
and opened the door. He stood slobbering over gray whiskers,
ears up, ready to roll in red collar and red tongue. See,
I keep a box of Ol' Boy treats on the desk, the very desk
where I planned to write somberly of Grace's sold remains,
the carnival atmosphere, my brother hawking sandwiches.
A brutal August morning, and I was drunk. I bid high
for Pirtle's kitschy phallic ashtray, his .410 shotgun, Grace's
nicest remaining quilt. Impressed with my cleverness,
I dumped the loot in the Chevy, shook hands, and wove
200 miles home, sipping whiskey in the car, the gun
leaning upright on the passenger seat. So, I intended

to mine these absurdities in depth, but the heavy breathing
continues. When I lift my head to the window,
Fudge, I mean Negrito, is folded on the step looking directly
in my eyes, as goofy, happy, and alive as anything
is likely to ever be again, indifferent to sabotaged stories,
an old woman's death, our parceled, discounted years,
my reckless stupidity. *It's all about biscuits*, he seems to pant.
I yank the door, toss the sky a handful. He labors up
and, slinging a halo of drool, lopes toward hope and glory.

Apologia for Epigraphs

> And in the dark carnival
> he masqueraded as a count,
> a proud man among beggars,
> with his little silver cane.

A start to conversation. Conceit to rise to.
Step stone to approach the situation differently.
Good advice. Wish, opening salvo, dinner
with guest of your choice. Oblique conspiracy.
Crutch, wrench, vase of ashes on the mantel.
Barrel of gun and first bullet. Pretense of learning.
Neruda the preferred company, of course.
Take this fellow of his, for example, his vanity,
hand raised to a worn hat as he passes
each alley, accepting, aloof, the totem and defense
of his preposterous cane. I am not saying
that this man is me, understand, nor you a beggar,
nor this long week our own dark masquerade.
I'm not implying I am hollow from my desire
to impress or that you'll be seduced by such puffery.
Nothing of the sort, nor any recent distractions,
nor a persistent, deserved cloud of blues
dimming the sky of an otherwise fair morning.
Merely suggesting these four lines appealed to me,
and I offered you to them—I mean, *them* to *you*—
in lieu of any better way we might begin.

Apologia to Every Woman I Ever Wanted

Impossible. Sacrament of failure. Received, doubtless,
as it ever was and ever shall be. Yet this morning,
bowed to a new week, I feel I might offer some token.
Acknowledge, perhaps, your disorienting power.
Or proclaim honestly I forgive you your arbitrary will,
demands of costly tribute. The cause of your distrust
I'm resigned to never knowing. And yes, as to matters
unspoken that night, between candle and sacrificed plate,
matters that eye and hand and even music failed,
it's those I regret, the unspoken I'd like back this morning.
While as to what harrowing rituals I did enact then,
testaments for which I "wined" feebly into position—
I believed every word. Even if you turned suddenly
from the table, dark and iridescent as you rose for purse
and the door. Even if, on more than one blessed occasion
I must confess, you took my startled hand and led,
in unearthly beauty, to the miraculous altar of your bed.

Apologia to a Woman's Ear

On a pontoon through Tortuguero Canal,
Mosquito Coast, beneath an insinuation
of sun after three torrential days,
I alternate my gaze from ear and neck
of the woman seated before me
to crocodiles lounging flotsam and beach
along edges of dark water.
The translucent fragileness
of neck curved like a vase, its porcelain delicacy,
downy trail. The croc's toothy grin
and depthless marble eye. Finally, the ear
takes all attention, its nature more
hypnotic, dangerous perhaps than jungle.
My head tired, feet torn, I am a man
on a boat on foreign water I recognize.
Sadness flourishes here, anger, disappointment.
Inappropriate, perhaps, to an airy tangle
blown free from a woman's
braid, prancing an ear now as exclamation,
now as question mark, now some other
signature of unknowable language.
The same wisp I touched
in the rain, tucked behind same small ear.
I am a man who believes, despite his mood,
that it is an intimate, devilish ear. A family lunges
fingers at more crocodiles, mean and sated,
voices rising. I keep staring at the ear,
imagine leaning forward, grazing
the pale neck, a man whose lips, freshly wetted,
part in a whisper of breath, of just the right words
to humbly accept its exquisite invitation.

Apologia for Cash and Luck

> And all those bloodstained men discovered their
> rank was the same: the earth has no adversaries.
> —Neruda

Slouched and heated beneath weight of luggage,
I arrived reluctantly to this country, advertised richness,
arrived sleepy, sad, disconnected, language rust.
Here's how I've constructed weeks—afternoons staring
across a frame of Guanacaste trees, grasping, to a smoky
cordillera. At night, bamboo creaks in the wind,
through open windows, pliant sails of an earthen ship.
In the mornings, like now, I rise early, heat a cup
of local coffee. I stare at my brown legs; I feel my heart.
Sun fires the leaves of papaya and banana saplings.
There's more here than idle nature, of course. On a table,
two admirable stacks of bills—385 clean US dollars,
a thick, ragged quarter inch of colones, 274,000 precisely.
Curtains whip the room. A salt shaker for weight,
an unlit candle. On a small pad, notes and conversions.
More than enough, as I tally, for the next launch
of desire and folly, enough for departure, for return,
enough for me, the living, perhaps the ravenous dead.

Apologia to the South of France for Nicaragua

> They rushed to Nicaragua.
> They disembarked, dressed in white,
> firing dollars and bullets.
> —Neruda

I've not forgotten your lavender fields, ripe cherries,
sculptured countryside of vine, long late dinners
of truffle, asparagus, rabbit, olive, buttery liver.
Your laughter and candled nights, orchestrated strolls,
your slender crystal legs. Your hot, gentle hands
of sun. Your breads and honey, your ocean, your art.
I've been faithful in my way to the dream of our future.
But by god, some tribal virus of Central America,
ancient contamination, pollutes my blood. Anoche,
mouthing a Chilean red with our seared corvina
and mashed plátanos, with the lights of Ciudad Colón
and its soccer field scoring the wet Mora valley…
Well, stories of a Nicaraguan paradise were told—
the next border, always the next border,
always a simple Indian people, dark and friendly,
resentful of neither bombs nor shopping malls.
But no bombs in Granada, no malls on lago paraíso.
(Who developed Granada, I asked, imagining
some Disney-thumbed blueprint. Well… "Spaniards,
homesick Spaniards, five centuries ago…")
A shady, coffee-studded hillside conquered now
for two months' salary; a year's buys a private island
dripping in thick green, my own monkeys.
Boat trip into town for groceries. You must admit,
Provence, even snarling, to a balmy, dangerous allure.
What shocks me, though, is not my usual fickleness,
but this palpable, culpable blood-tie I feel.
Remember, you weren't first: I betrayed Spain for you.

This is worse, I know. Patience. I'll return in time.
I'm almost certain that I will, almost absolutely certain
some remedy must exist for this beguiling fever.

Apologia to the Son of a Bitch
who Stole My Sandals on the Beach

By the time a wrinkled woman kicked sand at me
beside the spot and a man offered his flashlight
with advice "You can't leave anything,"
I was shaking my head. Besides, I didn't trust them,
by then shock had turned inevitability:
They looked like thieves, their dark families
and friends too, who eyed me as world's ripest rube.
Perhaps you had watched me chase crabs,
squint at Maxfield Parrish shades of pacific evening,
requisite rolled trousers, calming Cuba libre.
I hoofed the village barefoot, found every sharp angle.
Did I mention only by poor luck and circumstance
was I there at all, chewing on sunset
to recoup hotel and meals, that I'd no other shoes
or a dry shirt? I request: what sort of lowlife
steals a man's sandals? I dreamt of your dirty feet
in my leather and at morning returned
to study a sandy mash of prints. Partly yours,
no doubt, in fitted Corinthian straps that measured
continents. You've no idea. So I wish for you
gangrene, oozing leprous sores, charry stubs, the usual.
But no quick death. Rather, some simple truth—
say decades in your own paradise, hombre,
mortgaged ankle-deep to gringos, who buy a pair
any damned time they please. Walk a mile in those.

Apologia for Postcards

Shimmering seascape, island paradise,
rainbowed birds and flora, neat stack
already addressed to those I rarely see.
After a season in this succulent country
I leave tomorrow, and blank squares
await some quick scribble. Nothing profound,
nothing sacred or of lives we practiced,
days and nights. Just a flirt, redundant wit,
reminder you were on my list. Just a spray
of sea salt in the wound, trivial post
announcing our too-obvious farewell—
I was here and glad you weren't. At times,
though, I'd have appreciated the company.

II

Got on my dead man's suit
and my smiling skull ring,
my lucky graveyard boots
and a song to sing.

—Bruce Springsteen

•

Crimes, like virtues, are their own reward.

—George Farquhar

Apologia for My Father the Killer

He's young, lean, knotted,
immortal as I see him.
Here the sad business—one boot
on each rail of the shaft,
and as the flushed cow
ran blind beneath,
to bring the sledge down
hard between wide ears.
But when that ridge of bone refused,
it took a second blow,
or third as the beast screamed.
"*Hit* the bitch!" And as he stood down,
trembling, "You'll get used to it."
To which my father replied, "No I won't."

Apologia to War Emblem, "Dud as a Stud"

> Says Eisuke Tokutake, spokesperson for the Yoshida family, which purchased War Emblem last September for $17 million, "Clearly, this is not a good situation."

You're causing frowns in Hokkaido,
twitchy palms at Lloyds of London: Libido Lost.
War Emblem, equine brother, I am for you.
200 broodmares booked this year alone,
$70,000 lost for every "covering" you refuse.
At each chestnut haunch, twitch of sleek
tail, you look away, pretend not to see the rut
you're in. "Bird-watching," worried pros call it.
"It happens." Small consolation to the Yoshida
clan. So, tough. I peer into your dark eyes,
luminous and lonely, and think I know
precisely how you feel. Still a young stallion
at four, but your time on the hard track
of a fast run, sun high, money down,
that's all behind you now. Which is fine, too—
for peace, stillness, tender grass of home,
but not a sweaty, quivering parade of flank,
penetration on demand, nature's good lust
commodified for yen. It seems a lifetime past—
two minutes of destiny, a bugle blast,
that blanket of roses smelling, for one instant,
like heaven caressing the genius of your legs.

Apologia to Alan Dugan and Bill Shoemaker

> so stumble, heart, under the weight
> of heavy air and loss of teeth,
> hair, eyes, veins, arteries, balls and all,
> plus living memory.

You're dead for weeks before I hear about it,
and then incidentally and by chance.
So this October morning, Stella d'oro blooming
out of whack of season with a white sun
hot on arms and neck of my reasonable health,
I conjure you both and reckon some stupid
guilt over time unaware you're way ahead of me
into the ground. But it's not about me, it is?
Who gives a damn for the best horse
or best luck? It's 1986, dry clear afternoon
in Louisville and Ferdinand, at 17-1 and locked
behind 15 others, knocks the rail twice
before the first turn. But down the backstretch,
when a sudden magic space appears, man/beast
leaps for the dusty portal of that dream.
Or in the fixed verse of history, "Daylight
and victory. Roses and champagne. The Shoe
54 years old, and his beautiful third wife
shouting she loved him." That year, Dugan's 64
and writing *Poems Six*, his best. That year,
moreover, I move from Louisville and family,
leave my state poorly published, alone,
surely unacknowledged, hungry for what I might
make or destroy. But this isn't about me.
Nor what comes later, thundering, regardless.

Apologia for Missing Cousin Willie's Burial

> A race that gives suck to the maimed and crazed, that wants
> their wrong blood in its history and will have it.
> —Cormac McCarthy

Nothing to forgive now, and forgetting's
easily done. No services, no funeral home,
straight to the plot. They "planted" you
—a favorite phrase of my father,
who calls to lay out the common details—
on Wednesday before Thanksgiving,
and no one knows why they waited three days.
Maybe so kin could cipher the odd
Christian names the obit wore like a stiff suit
and figure was it really you. It was.
Alive, you scurried and scrounged for nowhere—
a forensic rotation of rape, robbery,
bungled murder, state and private addresses,
somehow lasting to 69, forever for our clan.
Dad surprised at how many of the kids showed,
even Berniece, crying, who hadn't
acknowledged her brother in years. Small wonder
though he hadn't known the cemetery—
nearly to the Larue line, down a thin neck
of Turkey Hollow at the poisoned end.
And my father, natural storyteller
and our last one, parceling out the sad
facts that we laugh about: the body delivered
by mini-van, in a plyboard box sprayed silver.
The top lifted for any of the family
who cared to see: there was Willie, skull back,
toothless mouth agape, pate the size
of perhaps a large citrus. The mottled crowd
quiet and cold at the site, but stepping away
when a tractor growled in to cut the hole.

Apologia for T., Five Years Gone

The lip of that puckered roof drip,
drip, drooling into an off-key bucket.
My friend bent low in a sepia field
has left the house for bad or worse,
snatches after a single dead-weight leaf.
Fingers slim and bent as rust-nails.
He succeeds, or fails, I wouldn't know,
he has turned a weathered back to me,
splashed crownless hat back into place.
The umbrella appears as premonition,
and from the secret of its blooming
falls a bottle, a bone, a trumpet.
Cracked pocket watch and a list of names.
My friend turns once to remember,
theatrical across the shoulder of his coat
as if this rain will surely never end,
then leans ahead in possibility of a bow,
a curse, soundless exit or assignation.
He slouches for fallen gypsy grass,
parted grains failed compass for the sky.

Apologia of the Traveler

Not stark black and white of romantic cinema—
from the first you recognized this city's
pervading theme of gray. Gray pitted streets,
gray pools of alleys, sooted gray stone
enclosing blocks of shuttered windows, each gray.
Yet how easily you lose yourself
in an area you thought you knew
by head, if not heart. So easy it's stunning.
A neighborhood I want to show you,
she explains, then leaves you roaming hours.
Statue of gray man mounted on gray horse
rises as axis above spokes of confusion—
averted gray glances, shoulders in gray coats
pinwheeling your body. Back to horse and man,
tumbling into another congested possibility.
When at last you find your friend
kneeling beside her tattered suitcase,
she doesn't look up from trinkets for sale.
You know she's boiling, has had enough of you
and your kind of foreign. The warted gnome
at the next stall ladles a plate of gruel,
fingers your dirty bills with contempt, and you
chew and chew on this hot mess. The city's smell
you can't capture, fear you'll never escape—
must of history and the whip, floated
on barge of refuse. Maybe not. An unnamable
peppery something of dreams and deaths.
But whatever it is never leaves the hair now,
clothes, skin. How to get home
is sudden urgency—who knows why you haven't
asked before. Air? Water? Fire? Who knows
why you came or the unforeseeable
route back. Back to what?, the captain smiles
from his toothless hole, punches your gray ticket.

Apologia to My Publisher for Replacing the Author Photo

Mea culpa, mea culpa: since the catalog
arrived I've come to loath that smug poseur.
His kindliness, tweed and black t.
In all, a man whose ass requires kicking.
New shot enclosed. It has its own issues—
apparent baldness (trick of sun),
angling branch above author's ear
like broken horn (deflected inspiration?),
overly cruel contrast of light and dark,
bleached features, disturbing anonymity
of chin (trick of shadow). Still,
woodsy setting feels right, and most gut
has been scissored discreetly into history.
I've come to realize a problem these
photos share—they look like me. Some more
than others, my friend. At least
forgiving smile gone. If arms akimbo
strike a calculated toughness, aloofness
convinces. Please grant this favor.
Immortality weighs, as long as the book's
in print. So if a switch is possible,
in name of god make it. Don't consign me
to life as that bastard. Whatever
time and money's involved, I'll pay in full,
every shekel, and thank you for the debt.

Apologia for My Addiction to the Thursday Horoscope

An event not to believe in, but to aspire to.
Not burdening crucible of the daily prediction:
that this afternoon I will "dance alone," alright,
but tonight's "emergence of a bold, new, extroverted
lover" too much pressure for rainy Sunday.
The weekly projection, though, moves me expectant
into week's end, blossoming week after.
Perhaps I agree a "reinvention of persona" is overdue
and make note to "inject wildness and badness"
into my behavior. Damn it, perhaps now *is*
the ordained moment to overcome fear and "reveal
my raw beauty to the world"! I feel ready, tense
but anxious at prospects of juicy serendipity,
pluckings of romance, wealth, wisdom that coming
days deliver to the prepared believer, harvests
of fate to eclipse past failures. I'm Aries, by god,
but why not "shed self-importance"—who needs it?—
for "goofy fun"? Maybe my big mistake really *is*
"a stroke of great fortune." As weekend dwindles
into Monday's office stumble, Tuesday's thunderous
hangover turns Wednesday unseasonably cold,
who in his rational mind wouldn't look hard
at Thursday's stars for some tolerable realignment?
Who isn't wild for "the mysteries of shape-shifting,"
to cultivate a "sly and renewed ambition"
with the eye of a fox, to read the future as his own?

Apologia for the First Day of School

I don't teach until tomorrow, Tuesday, yet
woke with an old cocktail of excitement, dread,
anxiety, knot in the gut. In my office,
a pale photo of my *first* first day—
stuffed like kielbasa into stained t-shirt,
strained inhalation of breath, peek over
the precipice, vintage cars surrounding
John J. Audubon Elementary. Mom had probably
walked me; this was traumatic for her, too,
her youngest and last stepping forward.
Each year, at the family table before Day One,
dad counted off years remaining (including
college—my brothers and I had no choice):
"Well, son, only 14 more years of school!"
"Only 11 years to go!" "Just another 9 years!"
The duration seemed unimaginable, a stone
I could barely drag, but I enjoyed the ribbing.
When he could leave early from a job,
dad would wait outside Prestonia Elementary,
my next school, in white t-shirt and pick-up,
an egg roll and sweet sauce, my favorite,
in greasy wrappers. I'd climb into the truck.
Well, classes or no, I can't focus today,
can't read, all those beginnings tugging.
I'll go to campus—watch the parade, summer tans,
ensembles, new books, make a show of organizing
my desk. None of us guessed I'd be here
thirty years later. No one waiting anymore.

Apologia for Stigmata

On page two of the syllabus, low and marginal
to in-class viewing dates, a fiery abstraction
blots the paper. I look away from text
and discover my left hand shiny and wet,
unbelievably, artificially red like dripping candy.
I announce to the group that "blood is seeping
from under my wedding ring, what can this mean?"
Some grunts, a vague laugh. The ring slips
easily over the goo. I rub its streaked
gold, then drop the mess into my shirt pocket
with a prayer it won't stain. Seconds stretch.
Mumbled recovery about "contemporary stigmata"
gets guffaws, a few. I wipe away the worst
with a cloth from my pocket, detect a tiny, angled
scar, aggravated burn from the broiler
browning day-old bread. Blood keeps coming.
I watch it balloon, break surface, divide
again around the wound to the palm. The room,
I notice, is silent. I daub the page, wrap naked
finger, resume speaking of themes to recur
in the coming months of Mondays: this comedian's
psychosexual angst, blurring of fantasy/reality,
question of whether, in an empty universe,
a moral life is possible. I'm a professional;
the money's secure. A spot of red surfaces
on white. I turn the handkerchief, clamp tight,
and keep explaining about the urgency
of our contract, preparedness, our timely arrival.

Apologia for "The Yolk of Marriage"

Please allow me to set the stage: I have cleared
my oak desk of all but two thick folders of essays,
two pens, one sharp pencil. This morning
I am to begin a week of hard, intensive grading.
I sip my cup, sigh, and open the first folder.
The top paper, a study of Rip Van Winkle's burden,
is titled "The Yolk of Marriage," and I know then
how morning and week intend to comport themselves.
Now, I am not one to collect student errors
for chuckles at parties, and I am not, in theory,
opposed to any honest ignorant mistake.
Hell, marriage *is* a runny, messy business, is it not?
I mark the essay, move it left to a completed
pile of one, and begin another. But when I read
of Roderick Usher "exercising his demon," I stop,
stare, decide to turn the calendar to October.
Last month's red panda and snow leopard exchanged
for mountain gorilla, chimp, and orangutan,
their forlorn, knowing faces. Outside, it is cold
for a t-shirt. I chew a length of champagne grapes,
dark and sweet as small blueberries. Note mums
full with purple flower. The sky, opaque.
I imagine my demon—sit-ups, chin-ups, sweaty, toned.
Neither of us, I believe, has much to add
to the pedagogical debate. When I detect my dog
limping, I go in, fill a hypodermic with Adequan,
inject his arthritic hip. When I return to the desk,
my fingers too are resistant and stiff, they too
at the mercy of years and some greater judgment.

Apologia for My Morning at the Milton Conference

Every two years, on a Friday in October, I arrive
late, disheveled for the plenary address, pleased
this day that by chance or fate I bear little hangover.
Current discussion details Augustine, et al,
concoction of Satan, from Old Testament tidbits,
into worthy Adversary, with attendant
subplots such as the illogic of goodness's
corruptibility and the impossibility of pinpointing
evil's beginning as it wriggles down its receding path.
Well, I believe that I follow most of this,
mostly, although I am distracted by the hatred I feel
for blonde hair, shaved nape, and herringbone shoulder
of the joker in front of me who leans further
and further sideways until I can make out
the Yale scholar at her podium only by tricking my eyes
to focus within the silhouette of his tilted head.
To my left, a twitchy young guy spends the hour
reading his own essay, "Conscience in *Lycidas*,"
blacking out lines and x-ing entire paragraphs.
To my right, the dean of my college, so I sip my coffee
quietly and try to look sharp in my Goodwill
sport coat and same formless slacks I wore yesterday
to class, and day before. Satan, meanwhile,
like the rest of us, remains misinterpreted,
explaining until he's blue in the face that evil
maybe isn't evil at all, but glory, and anyway what
choice about it? He just wanted respect he had coming,
not to play clown and yes-man to some upstart son,
and needs Eve, sweet Eve at least, to understand.

Apologia for Charley

Good year, that: your bungalow facing
muddied river, necklace of dog shit,
beer cans, stinking fish and bones
of Confederate boys. Barbeque pits rusted
in heavy rain, black mosquitoes rising.
My rooms on the other side, toward street
and empty field, maze of pathways
linking us, missing plank
in Bubba's fence, matching bottles of gin
large enough for one evening. Climbing
through the hole for two more.
Good nights, those: when I fell hard,
broke another glass, crawled the last
hundred yards of parking lot
to my door, ankle already doubling.
Fists on wall, knocks at 3:00 a.m.,
rising naked to answer. Limping for months.
Good mornings, too: coffee, hoarfrost,
requiem of mail and slow hours.
Afternoon stroll to your place, promise
of straight talk—women, books, money.
Fence's song at 4:45 p.m., bloody steaks,
fired potatoes, tomato juice in Mason jars.
How men eat. Every ghost who dropped by,
erudite and thirsty, loaded for fun.
When jackasses jacked the rent again,
plowed my field and my girl came to town,
I got out of there, packed away
good times. Soon enough, so did you.

Apologia to Gregory Hemingway

Fisher Prince—working marlin heavy and true
as Papa's pride. Sureshot—nineteen doves in row,
a boy your age. Hunter—black-and-white
squint, bigger guns, trophies. Even writer—
some of How It Was. Next-to-last time I saw you,
guest star at commemorative planting.
Mayor in cummerbund, prodding shovel
at edge of a forlorn twig. You standing almost
steadily in smile and flowered shirt, red face.
Your own kids later claimed it miracle
you too didn't pull the trigger, bow to ghosts
that danced you through life, miracle you persisted.
Though not such as to inspire $500 bail
before your heart wore out in a Dade County cell
the night before a judge's reckoning.
And last time I saw you, freckled paw
questioning the thigh of a blonde at an island dive,
star still of that skinny firmament of sand.
And Gloria, oh Gloria, how may I speak of you,
how should I presume? Hard words Pop wrote
only now exhumed, and that final night
on the lonely road of who you could never become—
high-heel straps in a fist, flowered dress
mangled on the arm, Miami heaven aglow across
your mutilated beauty. Crucifix of family tree,
the sheriff's flashers tolling in dizzy
bells of light. How we couldn't stop laughing.

Apologia for the Concerns of Literature

> ...I come from the campo, the countryside,
> and I believe that the most important thing is not man.
> —Lorca

By the time the acclaimed adaptation
of the heralded apocalyptic work
by the famous political playwright unfurled
its first act, we were all perched
at the TV on couch and chairs with a nice
syrah. I watched for awhile the Oscar-heavy
legends and handsome new faces
wince through sickness and confusion,
growl recognition at their corruptions,
wail at a wall of recrudescent world plague.
Pity and sacrifice, irony, waste, travail.
Compelling performance, superb
and erudite writing, ingenious craft.
At my epiphany that no other bottle
would be opened, I excused myself, went out
to stare at the koi pond and the moon,
waxing to full tomorrow. Unseen behind
hedge, dogs next door unleashed their full
unbridled plaintive fury at my presence,
and I smiled again at the bobcat
I'd seen near our house two days earlier,
in the clearing, and at my approach
its nonchalant grace as it stood, turned,
and leapt the rusted wire fence. From where
I stood, the windows flickered with
colors bled from the suffering screen.
Then I went back in to join my friends.

Apologia for America at War

I pass morning outside
in short sleeves,
forearms bare under March sun.
As I seal grain
with rags and fruitwood stain,
I wear protective gloves
to keep my hands pristine.
If plan holds,
this small table will balance
books, and drinks, for many years
in the room where I
control the world,
in a place reserved
beside my old chair,
its threadbare gold
concealed just today, in fact,
beneath a cotton throw—
all virgin forest, snow-blue peaks,
grizzly as broad as the sky.

Apologia for Voting

> It is the duty of the patriot to protect his country
> from its government.
> —Thomas Paine

Member card in hand, easy target before
the table unfolded in the grade school gym,
I asked how, oh Lord, had I arrived
at this moment on otherwise fair afternoon
of a tolerable fall. Smiles all around—
the dutiful zealot, the satisfied citizen,
the rube. The congratulatory glow
as the woman checked my name. I signed.
An eager fellow escorted me to the curtain.
I didn't run. I stood bravely
in that penumbra of space for a duration
I hoped appropriate to soulful contemplation.
I pressed it, the button the well-intended
had convinced me times demanded,
parted drapes to more approving smiles.
As I hurried for the lot, children unseen,
unheard, I folded the sticky flag
meant to announce the act. I took the sun's
heat on my neck, recalled a woman
who'd sued the Red Cross for allowing
her to drive too soon after a blood-letting.
I circled out, offering a silent prayer,
a sad, thankful declaration: count me
with cynical poor who know better, count me
with apathetic youth, count me with patriots.
The highway aimed toward my private
woods, I thought how I loved this country
too much to ever betray it again.

Apologia for the Storm as It Arrives to Us

The splintered boats, pancaked houses,
highways north clogged with exodus,
the telephones that ring on without answer—
these are distant abstractions,
headlines already history. Cross-legged
on the porch, sufficiently under cover
so that rain may not mar my pristine volume,
I am reading of Henry James' visit
to the Union wounded at Portsmouth Grove,
his discomfort at their silence, watchful
eyes, hacked and exploded young bodies.
According to the narrative, he ferries home
of two minds, silent, guilty, anxious
for the comfort of his room and books.
I hold my right hand lightly above the page,
follow the lines, feel the texture
of fine paper. Over the voice of the author,
I hear wind in our trees, no threat,
barely force to whip and whisper limbs.
I feel mist on my lowered face, retreat more,
and, hand holding place, look up
into easy rain, the gloaming. We're back
to school, anxious for cooler days.
Our lawn and leaves dark, luminous, stained.
No more light now for books and less
each moment. I read on, however dangerous.

Apologia for an Autumnal Moment

> at that purple hour when all the crows go hoarse
> and sail off to the crags and the black eaves...
> with nectar gathered from a hundred flowers
> and the hundred sorrows of the gathering dark.
> —Don Paterson

After each tender phrase, or line that harrows,
she looks up from the book open on her legs,
looks across patchy lawn, tumbledown leaves
congregated about each solitary trunk,
into wedges of light refined by branches
as if to release this interior world through
her gaze, connect it palpably to hard exteriors,
the real world, breath and blood and pulse,
and cast it loose. When, again, words turn her
face upward toward a living hour, the western sun
of these short days blinds her. Instinctively, she
raises a hand as shield, then lowers it
to squint into something, suddenly, very much
like audacious perfection: the bordering road
deserted and silent, low verse of cicadas,
the torch, so warm, alien and distant.
Through arms of slanted light, something falls,
something sparkles from above: motes of sky,
or casings of nut solved by unseen squirrel.
And always unnamable tendon, the elusive other...
She holds it, waits. But what to do with
a moment caught in a world beautiful and lost?
When she next looks up, the sun is as expected
restrained, and the day, resumed in motion,
though fair, no longer perfection by any means.

Apologia for a Common Sabbath

Faint holiness, just sufficiently imbued
to skew hours to troubled unease, curtail
trails of profit. Calendar-common, redundant
enough but for its pungent air,
the air a soft milk ladled between trees,
the trees jeweled with webs,
the webs a sticky tiara to unbowed head.
By then the finery of this language, too much,
indulgent, fails to find you on your knees,
knees of trousers sodden with mud,
down in the muck of the way you like it,
arms lifting the rot of a dead season,
the succulent goo, refused unguent of the fallen
and composted, as, again, conceits drop
wide of the mark. But as you look up, cold neck,
suit of leaves, patchy complaints
and revenges muttered to violated silence,
or rather as you don't, something might step
from that barrier of woods, an imminent wildness,
step alert from the uncleared
to acknowledge you bent to your work
of polishing a secular square of dirt,
step to show itself, vain, vanquished,
horns raw, claws torn, coat matted with stink,
promise, threat, step unconquerable from fog.
But nothing does, again, and then it's night.

Apologia to Anne Sexton

> So I tried to be delightful to Anne Sexton,
> and a lover of life (which I'm not),
> and I drew her this diagram of the story of Cinderella:
> —Kurt Vonnegut

Not an unusual morning tableau for our cabin
in the woods: I'm perched on closed commode
with mug of organic shade-grown coffee,
good steaming cup, looking down on my wife
in the bath with hers. She is filling me in
on her night at the theatre, grading dinner
at my favorite restaurant. Here is the thing:
She has placed your book on the tub's
edge, so to speak to me without distraction.
When I glance at you, intentionally grainy
as if sizing me through a screen, your face
is a watery mess: gash on cheek, long tear
in one eye, drip precisely from mouth's edge,
tourniquet at forehead. I am trying to follow
the politics of the play but am disturbed
by your pretty, upside-down, clear-eyed sadness.
Wounds of water, not blood, but I have to
do something so swipe at them, smear the cover
of this volume of dwarfs, wolves, ovens,
worsen your suffering. Then, dunce though I am,
I do what I should have done: lift the book,
turn it, and dry your face on the wool of my leg.

Apologia for Waking in Hell

Canny speculum of same warm house,
same cotton shroud over your head.
Duplicates of soft slippers that perfectly
hold your bony feet.
Smell of buttermilk waffles,
your favorite, crisping on griddle,
and a beautiful woman singing of playful love,
flashing auburn hair.
Picture-true reproductions of your books,
your skulls, your masks, your shells.
Mantis on window, bowed
south. Outside, a world of unerring similacra
and clear winter light you worshipped.
Something like breath floats
from your mouth as a single yellow flower,
your favorite, raises its thin neck,
parts, and dies. Crow lands
hopping on one leg, frames you in a dark eye
and begins to laugh forever.

Apologia to the Moment before My Death

The instant could involve a bridge, stuck pedal,
crush of steel and no languor for reflection.
Or foreign landscapes might supply a scenic stage,
some natural magnificence of glacier, coast or sky.
Perhaps children will sit rhyming at the fire,
a tender living hand trace and complete my own.
But I doubt it. I know now, in this December
moment, the room will be sparse, last sunset
an irony of discounted, billboarded, exit-ramp defeat.
Trucks will blare the onset of night as I wait,
alone with hollow escaping breath
and the taunt of each petty shadow. I will
raise a toast to us then, a man prematurely old, adjust
blinds just so and leave them wide. The ice,
the ice, the ice will clink once in a final diminished
chance, and I will raise the glass, and I will
close eyes to darkness and to dust and speak
with the soft distinction of a father back to this,
this precise, ineluctable moment of waste and want,
"Bastard, what were you possibly thinking?"

Apologia to Renaldo, and Goodbye

On two deck chairs positioned on my single
deck, in flamingo-blaze dawn of rum and Scotch,
this as close to speechless perfection
as men like us will ever come. Patented grin
on your dumb fatuous face as you slumped aside,
blood a sacrament on your lips
and I so drunk I fell over you—
that's how it was, how you were, how I was,
and I crawled back crying already,
and blood, blood a child's popsicle, blood as blood.
The emerald passage of your eyes said at once yes,
don't worry, be well, you were fine
my friend and now it's yours. I couldn't see
anything then but blur, feel except for
weight on my arms and storm. And goodbye
to you, amigo, as in god be with you, goodbye.
There be no angels now to take thee.
I was dizzy drunk, Rey, staggered for the phone.
And for nothing plus nothing it's worth, goodbye.
That dawn, paragon of beauty. I'll remember.

Apologia for the Highway Dead

Those two extremes in their passing—
one of black clot, exploded fur,
jellied guts no longer justifying guilt.
And second sort, the freshly slain,
lean discarded refuse, turned
neck, tall ear, perhaps only unnatural
twist of foreleg proof she's not napping
until all frost burns away.
Before I empty paper cup of coffee
with reminder from Bāsho to daily count
the morning glories, I pass seven bodies
and quit counting. We witness each,
carry the load or not, piston
deeper through dynamited hills.
Pal, I have taken this road all my life
and keep driving, drive forever
with my cup, crushed sack of treats,
fearless nonchalance to nagging ghosts.
I know these curves, every one,
and drive until the sun, blinding east,
clears the window, passes me, flares
again at the finish and dies.
Twilight, its panicked peripheries,
this time of year is most dangerous.
We pretend vigilance, nervous few, lunge
humming and distracted for the dark.

Apologia to the Last Full Moon of the Year

> In each thing there is an insinuation of death.
> Stillness, silence, serenity are all apprenticeships.
> —Lorca

I submit to you tonight as I have
on many nights these thirty-eight
years, nights when you reveal
and are revealed, when I sit
without complaint within the private
jurisdiction of my longing,
and they are never enough or suffice.
Tonight, you paint my legs pale
in the hot water of this sauna
and ask me nothing. I remember
January, our year opened; now neither
gains nor losses seem unbearable.
A stranger from the city
carried his lens as great around
as a Yule log, landed it on this patch
of earth I roam like a pirate.
We stood, all of us, in the dark,
drunk and shivering, plying
inverted Pleiades, rings of Saturn,
retreated Mars, a hazy Northern galaxy,
your own hook of crater, shadow.
But I like you big and round,
like you to myself, like now,
this bluish sky, this blush of cloud
curling to announce you over me.
You can have me any night you want,
as long as we can, until I make
a brilliant, senseless widow of you.

Apologia for the Bone Box

Modest interest turned hobby,
turned grotesque. Shelves crowd
with the bleached splinters
of the animal dead, spell of claw
and joint, socket and skull
gathered from path, wood, verge
over a dozen countries and years.
This and that. I considered
beginnings, "When I became a child,
I put away manly things," or
"One needn't collect bones, bones
collect you," that sort of folly,
opted for simple confession:
We need less gloom in the room,
more light, less hell, more laughs.
I snag a box from the heap,
know its dimensions exact
for what fragments remain.
Fragile as eggshell, heavy
as stone. I layer deliberately,
bone china inherited in a will.
Not every piece, of course.
As promise of new ways, I hold back
the goat head lowered from
barbwire crucifixion—lopsided
erosion of beached hull,
divining compass of sloped horn.
As warning of the old—sturdy jaw
not unlike an ass, ferociously
toothy, contoured to the hand.
A gravy boat, a soup ladle.
The box I'll inter, mark with "X"
that spot we'll shovel forever.

Apologia for the Last Word

Your ambitions ran short
and you gambled all currency.
A house is a shell without voice
and the few you loved,
who loved you, left the world.
Gone too the red oak,
felled by storm or sweat
while you were somewhere else,
believing something else.
The past a pale line
of transgression, the future
a photograph of blindness.
Warblers remind of morning,
unseen on stillest branch
beneath sun whose time is noted.
Maybe you cared enough
to make losses matter,
maybe you did not and could not
and neither made a difference.
Maybe the sky is the color of sky.
With a last rattled breath,
last day, hour, instant,
what more did you have to say
and who remained to listen?

III

The partridge loves the fruitful fells,
the plover loves the mountain.
The woodcock haunts the lonely dells,
the soaring hern the fountains.
Through lofty groves the cushat roves,
the path of man to shun it.
The hazel bush o'erhangs the thrush,
the spreading thorn the linnet.

Thus every kind their pleasure find,
the savage and the tender.
Some social join, some leagues combine,
some solitary wander.
Avaunt, away, the cruel sway,
tyrannic man's dominion.
The sportsman's joy, the murdering cry,
the fluttering gory pinion.

—traditional

Apologia for the Indifference of Animals

Picking at trash along the southeastern edge
of property, I strayed farther and farther
from the protection of my ride, its throttled lure.
Understand: November sky low and thick in marsh,
a toddler's discarded drinking cup,
cigarette pack dissolved into sludge
when touched. Dressed cleanly, you see, for work,
I held the mess at arm's length, conscious
of early traffic and how it might unkindly perceive
a man bowing along the periphery.
So it was only suddenly and dipping in flight
that the red-shouldered hawk, raised
from low branch at my obvious approach,
surprised me. Naturally I stopped, straightened myself
beneath slow stride of wings, rust of tail,
dotted umber of heavy autumn vest.
He or she closed itself into next clump of hackberry
and oak, gave me its back as it resumed
the work of compact storm. I stepped forward
along the plank of shoulder, rotted tear
of blue notepaper in one hand, indecipherable phrases
of love or instruction. Understand, I moved
toward the distance of that dark shape.
Engines grinded past as I approached, drivers staring,
I suppose, at a man staring into bare woods,
or each squinted ahead toward some private sum.
When I crossed an invisible point, when I was
near enough, again wings expanded to slender points
and the dark eye ignored me as it rose.

Apologia for a September Garden

Each morning now, as early hour
radiates through each yellow branch,
I stand alone in our garden—
withered hosta, shrunken hydrangea,
shriveled coleus, black fern.
I stand alone with my hose
amidst budless chrysanthemum,
lopped beds of iris, brittle tops
of lily. Each day this month
an affront of blurring heat,
in which I stand, damp and stiff, pale
calves on offer to mosquito
and neck to last dizzy wasp.
Each morning since my wife left
I stand dutifully, sprinkle the dead
and dying, day ahead and
night passed. Since then,
I've not seen again the deer
at edge of wood behind our shed,
not the bold, inquisitive doe
nor her skittish buck, his pale
spotted hide, small horns she perhaps
finds beautiful, irresistible,
no longer watching me as if they could
hear already guns in season,
as if rough tongues, thirsty for salt,
tasted already their brief time gone.

Apologia for a Bat

We might yet agree that the day
remained the day as bat executed
its first startling circle
at edge of lawn. Yes, always woods
close first, then the sky
turning her gray shoulder,
but the bat exposed
in seizure of loops and reverses,
lost to us in curtains of limbs,
then crude flapping again visible.
As goldfinches glowed at late supper,
robins stroked gracefully
overhead, the bat hurtled
ecstatic variations
while we stood amazed, faces raised
and eyes troubled—
night undoubtedly nearer, silhouette
and its strange purpose,
black wings drumming closer
to our heads, then away, then closer.

Apologia for Separateness

Yesterday I held two wild lives.
I'm a known chump for birds,
am likely to declaim aureate glow
of chickadee's breast
or its precise, immaculate beauty.
It survived a smack in glass
and flapped from my porch without note,
only single fluid drop of shit.
The other, more complicated.
I knew the gestures—head twisted
to expanded feathers, eyes lidded—
but couldn't answer their appeal.
Trembling softness weighed nothing.
I heard a call from somewhere
out there in trees, arranged seed
beside parted beak and waited.
The moon glowed in daytime sky.
I'm chump for the wounded,
anything conformed to need.
Cardinal righted itself, shuddered, died.
This morning, October sun lay hot
on forearms and calves, collar and face.
I sat at edge of the same porch.
Much was restored—cardinal
buried under mulch, chickadees chattering
after thistle. Heat felt fine to me,
forceful, affectionate, healing.
I told myself to relax. Sit still.
Enjoy this being alive. But I couldn't, quite.

Apologia for the Fish I Overcooked on Good Friday

Simplicity: rubbed with oil, salt to taste.
Fundamental belief: such flesh to be served
rare, red inside, tender. So why this breakdown
not of skill but possibly character? Coals
glowed with fine, low heat. I tasted my wine,
squinted through trees crossing late sun.
Holiday incidental. Trust me: nails
and risings exalted here drive private penance.
So table set, beautifully, companion
awaiting my call, spring day vibrant and clear.
I knew from experience the fish's yielding
firmness, even by sight. Yet I waited.
Raised glass again to lips. Turned,
peered again at sky flaming to western conclusion.
The moment held, dimmed. The rest common:
side dishes pointless, cost and effort wasted,
fish gray and dead. I coughed complaints
with each dry swallow, dropped the rest to the dog.

Apologia to the Trout at Meadow Farm

I am thankful today for thumb and finger
chafed raw from lifting you, each blood-
dripped iridescent figure, between saws
of teeth and under cheek, laying each
in a lidded bucket atop twisted, wide-eyed
brethren. Small discomfort sufficient
to remind of dark pellets of rain ceased,
sky parted to sun. I demonstrated
once the proper wrist in an open-reel cast,
hooked hungry soul on deception
of retreating fly, reeled. Lesson complete,
involvement accepted, I devoted energies
to net, to freeing tangled barbs
from torn mouths and tongues, tried to hold
bodies still as the women laughed.
Later, we ate your fresh and tender flesh,
grilled, coarsely salted, the cold wine
succulent river of our gathering. 27 deaths
had been scrubbed from hands, mostly;
my gray trousers, darkly spotted, dried.

—for Larry Mapp

Apologia to the First Snake of the Year

One should have weighed the premonition
of your appearance, not shrugged symbolism
as myth, hearsay. Look how spring passes,
unraveled to temptation and dumb risk.
I did welcome the surprise of your composure
at the edge of our garden this morning,
admit your short length, pattern of drab scales
still argued portent worth listening to.
The slit of your eye seemed to recognize
I needed good advice about women and men.
But how to augur your vigorous evasion
as I approached and bowed, wide berth given
fig sapling, belly rustle, tail vanished
into stalks of spiderwort, blooming now
themselves toward narcotic, honeyed mischief.

Apologia to the Victims of the Storm

> "We won't never move. That'd mean Nature won."

Yesterday, I crossed safely your twisted lines,
bodies of trees, passed boarded windows
where old tend dim rooms of what you deserve
versus what you get. Through brief reprieve,
lull before next lash of punishment, good citizens,
survivors, ignite saws, roll anxious sleeves,
ladle soup for the stunned. Cameras are ecstatic.
Only sometimes does a man stop the work
of restoration, stand still at a truck bed
to ponder God's awesome will. Our losses, smaller,
buy no headline or sympathy. I sit half-attentive
to Chopin's delicacy, half to thunder firing
the sky's revived, careless attack. Our garden,
a tatter of dreams. Soon, I will move to the back
of this house that failed finally, aim light
at a puckered ceiling crying beside a bed.
Empty a bucket or two. Then I will pull on boots,
a low hat, and join you all in this mess of lives.

Apologia to the First Full Moon of Spring

I listened to what you had to say—
your assessment no different
than any faint and plaintive nightsong,
wind brushing any still-barren tree.
I watched you luxuriate and tease
from behind a comfort of black cotton,
flash your pure naked circle
so bright I almost couldn't look.
But I did. Until you began to rattle
in your kingdom or my eyes faltered
into tricks of light and distance.
Shadows on your skin created no face,
no island I might countenance.
Tulips, on conceits of fragile necks,
couldn't get enough of you, but I
began to tire of your reflection,
your tireless, tried admonishments.
Tire of explaining to a stone in the sky.
I left you, undressed for bed. Just
as I lay between our soft sheets,
the storm they had predicted, arrived.

Apologia for a Simple Restorative

Your failures are your own.
The sun is not ironic,
the wind this morning
acknowledges neither your silence
nor your shame. Shadows sparkle
on the saturated earth.
Moss gives beneath feet,
then responds, leaves no trace
for the human eye.

Apologia for Rain

I had harbored ambitions for what remained
of morning, black conceit for unveiling,
was exercising with a book of the dead
until I had my breath contained.
That's when rain began, rain we've dreamed
for weeks, me and starched grasses
and fractured earth, every suffering thing.
As it slapped roof and gutters,
landed a million sizzling kisses against
a graveyard of bone traced in limestone
beneath a shroud of leaves, et cetera,
I couldn't concentrate anymore on loneliness
or remember, quite, my plan for success.
So I opened windows, took a swing on the porch,
nosed further into the dead and their regrets.
I couldn't stop smiling: the chirps
and tiny motors of hummingbirds haloing his head,
cooler breath of fall on his arms,
this simple, mortal fellow nearly content
in a faithful life. Even the sun returned modest,
not red-haired bully bent to ravage
my own fine darkness, but a buddy after a nap,
luminous in heaven, nothing to do, lucky.

Apologia for the Martini Glass

Only your worst skeptics, in wounded dream,
denigrate the questing, open mouth
so willing of that first sublime frothing splash.
Only sorriest cynics, turned in wanting,
note not placid arctic surface of your beckoning
but rather tumultuous, slopping storm
of their own across-the-room inadequacies.
Designed more to spill than to contain,
spouts one. Your divinity and ascendance,
public devotees insult to all Darwinian reason,
argues another. But even they, the doubters,
league of unwilling, unable, uncool,
acknowledge sexy stiletto neck, cold allure
like nothing else in life between trembling fingers.
Better still on tongue, as they raise your lip
nervously but irresistibly to theirs—*ahh*—
only then lift eyes to lonely mirrors,
adjust crimson scarf, cocked dismissive eye.
In the century's grainy distance, a trumpet weeps—
Paris, 1925, the amber shadows of gaiety,
love's bite never clearer or more modern.

Apologia for a Martini in Winter

Imagine our bearded hero, larded
for the season, crouched in wide-wale cords
and an old warrior of a denim coat
beside a hissing yellow confetti of flame
hot in the belly of a Mexican fire pot.
The night sky clear; Pleiades bright-eyed
and flirty. Who may explain, then,
breach of martini between thumb and finger?
Any dullard cringes at the apish behavior,
the flaw of character in the frame.
Cold-hearted gin wobbles on slender heel,
sloshes dry seductions around a big mouth
and wonders where the party is.
Our fellow raises, steadies, puts lips
to his embarrassment. But where the sturdy inch
of Scotch obviously required, its muscles
of peat, salty North Sea solitude?
Who in his right mind attempts to align
the unalignable, marry swank and mirror
to isolated taupe, to winter tide,
stoic tongue wet for some luscious other?

Apologia for a Frozen Surplus

The connective tissue, method to the madness, listen:
By day three we had carved the holiday carcass to bone,
shred and tendon. No one moved from the table.
Enough delicacy, I decided, gave Tate flannel to warm her,
hammered every style of homebrew down Saul's throat.
I couldn't stay still or shut my trap; my head danced.
Then, since Saul and I had discussed on the long
highway from Fiery Gizzard State Park, apropos of nothing
save to muzzle silence, his dislike of goat meat
and since by some bizarre serendipity I had recently
bought (with cash) several pounds of prime goat tenderloin
from the rear of a van in a deserted parking lot
from a man named Ruple I'd never met (1-917-EAT-GOAT),
this seemed choice evening to fling wide the door
of my overweighted, top-loading freezer and reveal all.
My neatly taped brown-paper packages of goat, my stack
of rabbits, my quart of duck fat frozen pure as snow,
my bags of edamame (in and out of shell) and blackberries,
my bries en croûte, organic butter salted and unsalted,
spicy pesto, squid salad, tetnanger hops, leg of lamb
and three racks, handmade smoked salmon tortellini, etc.
I've been moody lately, distracted, eat nothing but
cold cuts, tomato soup, martinis. Even well lit in
the whispery glow of the open freezer door, cataloging my
dominance as hunter and gatherer, my mastery of technology
and international economic forces, I sometimes feel
queasy behind the pride, a twinge in the confidence.
But I stood before them anyway, glorified in my bounty,
hand extended like a grinning starlet dangling
her *Price Is Right* grand showcase—the car, the cruise,
the new luggage, everything yours if you guess it right,
come closest to our cost without going over. Tate
was fighting for breath and Saul sat stiffly silent.
As I held the door and nodded, he never opened his mouth.

Apologia for Cooking

> Here are grunions at their best.
> —James Beard

For Monday birthdays, Italian in full regalia—
veal chops painted in pale butter, seared with grapes
and sherry vinegar; handmade pappardelle with parsley
from the garden, topped with international
envoy of fresh shitakes, baby 'bellos, and the star,
the flirt, irrepressible *boletus edulis*, or *funghi
porcini, prodotti tipici,* sautéed simply in diced shallot
and white wine—chardonnay admittedly but
of unusual wit—finally pasta and 'shrooms perfumed
with black truffle virgin oil from the lips
of your coveted flask. To the side glass—left for you,
right for her—a 2000 Centine unassuming as old Tuscano
itself. Next day, after unfair dreams, you're back,
quick walk, review of values and resolves
during hot tub turn in bubbles, and onto Tuesday
anniversaries and French position—returned to the garden
to scissor thyme and rosemary from between stones,
rack of lamb messaged with Dijon mustard-bread jacket,
carré d'agneau à la moutarde, then that peasant
pleasure *haricots verts* but tumbled with wicked
flirtation of ginger before pairing of toasted almonds,
then: the showpiece: double-baked Yukon golds,
smashed with butter and cream and milled black pepper
and, again, liberal douse of truffle infusion
and spooned like babies into sturdier Idaho baker skins
—latter's flesh divided between bin and dog—
before topping of skillet-seared slices of foie gras,
shaved truffle, flowering drizzle of still more oil.
For libation you may ask modest forgiveness—not French,
but more-than-presentable 1997 Alexander Valley Zin

from Sausal's private reserve. It comports itself
in complex company. And now, places determined,
candles lit, your song low and luminous. Perhaps love's
on wing, perhaps October breezes blow just right.
Perhaps in any case the world's yours, time's now—
to extend a chair to your partner in life, to sit at last,
take a weight off, and stuff your storied guilt.

Apologia for a Thanksgiving Pissed Away

Afternoon lambent on the porch,
striving on the swing together.
Inexcusable warmth and bounty.
Scores of robins prodding mulch.
All day we couldn't help ourselves:
Battle of Brussels Sprouts,
Cranberry Crusade, the Great
Eggnog Debacle. Over and again,
our botched efforts at appreciation,
our strained care. Remembering
discarded offers from family
and friends. All across morning
into longer hours, passing each
in the looming space of our home.
Bedroom, kitchen, den, to the dining
table, foolish in candlelight,
oblique above gilded rims
of champagne. Laps of linen.
A toast with only ourselves
to thank. And our frail old dog,
making the best of us, sad but game
with the scraps we handed down.

Apologia for a Shopping List

Low-fat milk and a dozen
free-range eggs. I squeezed
the bread, six-grain,
announced it still as giving
as a woman's thigh
and soft enough to eat.
Our bed restored and tucked.

On the table, a vase of yellow
mums, and these lines,
wantonly assembled,
to wish you home today,
to wish you home today,
wish you home today
my love, to this empty house.

Apologia for Tuesday Bachelor Dinners

> "Every pig has his St. Martin."

When his wife's away on a wine evening with friends,
her lawyers and realtors, he is not playing rounds
of phone-patty with an ex or bellied at the trough
of a bar busting with action. No, he's long ago traded
sex for tradition—not the worst, the pig's feet
and fried squirrel, possum dumplings, mountain oysters,
but the bad enough—the fried chicken and catfish,
ham hocks and beans, butter-thick biscuits with sorghum.
Yes, tonight it's neck bones in a slow-cook crock
with kraut and sweet onions, meat smell maddening
the dog all day, then the man home and a skillet
of cracklin' cornbread as sop. It occurs to him,
as he motors through the rainy morning, that yesterday
and today are the *matanza,* the pig killing festivals
of rural Spain. A suitable serendipity. He recalls,
wheeling between brown fields, past residual livestock
into rising developments, his father regaling him
with childhood killing days in Larue (Lay-rue) County,
Kentucky, community come together to slaughter,
sear, butcher, salt, hook, hang, drink, eat. For years
he intended to ask the old man, a born raconteur,
to spin it again, and this time he'd pay attention.
He never did, though. And, anyway, he's often drunk
by the time these Tuesday fêtes bend the table.
The whole shameful, greasy mess gets slopped untouched
to the bin. When I raise my own fingers, they stink
of sauerkraut, just like, curiously, the man's in the poem.
The only part of a pig you can't eat, sir, is its oink.

Apologia for Private Drinking

> Take a broken whiskey bottle,
> set it on top of your head
> and dance. You have a costume,
> you have meaning.
> —David Ignatow

Begins as anticipation, as joy, circle
drawn to enclose the day. For example,
a man on a hammock, face burned red
from labor, supplicant over a book
broken across his lap. Sometimes, he will
look up at buttery wedges of light
striping lawn, dog sprawled and panting,
small animals come from the woods
for evening feed—rabbit, squirrel, finch,
each purposeful, contained. He will reach
a hand through chains securing him
in space, reach for a stem of crystal,
cold clarity. Begins, that is, as dream.
Canvas of dream. Ends as thumbed photo
of man as goat, beast's crooked dancing.

Apologia for Public Drinking

That is, explanation, or even, consideration,
but no more apologies today. It's spring,
it's spring, and I have concluded my morning
garden round. Nearly every hope is returned—
day lily field, irises on thick scapes,
cherry tree and blackberry, new lilac,
bed of poppy. An oozing, effusive testimony.
So no apologies. Even silly racket
of birds feels good. But what of drink?
Well, what of it? My intake doubles, triples
impressive limits when I am in the group.
Sure, I noted the noted guest's deflected gaze
as I concocted my next, but not my last,
potion of the party. You know from experience
I could write a tome, a virtual masterpiece,
on the blurry continuum of days, sirens of guilt,
aesthetic of destruction and endurance.
Theories abound for such behavior, how
explorers as we are born, courage bred.
Each theory nonsense and absolutely correct.
With onslaught of evening, come and see.

Apologia for Full Manly Vigor

Mess with my house, you're dead.
Sniff downwind at my woman, I'll disembowel
you and your children and little Aunt Sadie.
Think randomly about my dog,
we'll take turns pissing in your skull for eternity.
My folks? Don't even unfold a map
that might even contain the state of Florida
or you'll be ankle-deep in ashes and woe.
Otherwise, have a nice day or a shitty one.
Just don't come around. We're mowing grass
with a pitchfork. We're tossing salad
of thorns and vinegar, igniting pitchers
of kerosene margaritas, grilling dynamite.
It's Cinco de Mayo, Derby Day, garage sale
of rusty-edged trouble. It's any damn thing
I want it to be. This is domestic bliss
on Carcinoma Lane, in Battlefield Estates,
and I'm the original Señor Don't-Fuck-With-Me.

Apologia for Erotic Photography and a Woman Bathing

My wife sings from the other room, splashes,
inquires if I will visit. I linger over fleshy
favorites, then close Jan Saudek's *Eros*
and replace it on the art shelf discreetly between
the Prado's guide to collections, a Matisse
retrospective, a brochure of the Flemish Masters—
Rubens, Jordeans, and best, Van Dyck.
I step to the next room, irritated at myself
for unseemly irritation, and in a childish conceit
pretend that I have been summoned from valuable
work time. In a tub of fading suds,
a real woman, nicely shaped, draws a razor
in steady, even furrows down a raised leg. I drink
the last coffee, watch her finish a thigh
then lather and shave beneath each arm. I can't
think of an earthly thing to say not about me
or my complaints. Then I remember her telephoning
her ill grandmother, the conversation
that interrupted my brilliant concentration
as I tried to read. I inquire how she is, close
my eyes, open them, and listen for an answer.

Apologia for My Wife's Sleeplessness

Red meat. Char-grilled lamb chops of Sunday;
last night's rare sirloin. Or, copious blood
of Christ—French—taken lately by the case.
Regardless, she makes sure I know about it—
box spring wheezing, mattress quaking, comforter
cursed and discarded. She drops once, twice, thrice,
four times to complement of grunt and sigh.
I believe I have been ripped to the conscious world
on purpose, easy dreams culpability enough.
At last: mound of quilt, blanket's breath, quiet.
Restlessness other than gastronomic, perhaps.
I've no chance to ponder guilt, however,
as in a moment the theatre of sleep goes dark again,
stage lights rise, and I am strolling a Paris
arrondissement new to me, stopping at the window
of my destination, tiny bookstore/brasserie
"Vita." It is afternoon, summer and sunny;
I am alone but rigid with expectation, hungry.
Rainbows of volumes rise glowing to the ceiling.
Four precise, flowered tables promise future
intimacy. The tall hostess, all leg and Parisian
hauteur, opens the door, and I inquire in my best
if I may, if she pleases, peruse her *menu du jour.*

Apologia to the Red Planet

Again dark house, again silence.
After tumult fractured blessing. In the east
by south-east by the compass of the eye,
red diamond, mistaken once as beacon, or warning,
ship from universe grander than two small
beings in embrace of hurt on private post
of rock according to science not still but spinning.
This pink phantom in heaven perhaps all
that it suggests, fantasy and surety,
closer, they claim, than ever again for us,
closer each day for another few, surface deadly
despite appearances to any distant point-of-view.

Apologia for Morning Fog

Nothing unusual here—man leading dog
or vice versa. The dog sashays with the care
and close-shouldered effort of an old dog,
not abandon of the young and invincible.
The man notices this, notices how lousy
and old he too feels, a wreck nearly entirely
of his own making, not hammer of time.
Nothing strange about it, nor cicadas crowding,
nor light suffused, nor single small rabbit
bolted. Except that morning is wet
with fog, heaven's white apprehension, as if,
if the man allowed the conceit, which he does,
he approached some judgment of his life.
Webs everywhere, spun through night,
in air, on earth, trembling beauty and danger.
Each pattern briefly, exquisitely relieved.
The future's out there, no doubt of that,
nothing new. Man and dog turn together
toward a slow return. No reason to hurry it.

Apologia for My Dog's Happiness, with a Motif of Chekhov

Insouciance. A goofy, grinning pant.
Our late roughhouse, interlude
of a few hours' rest, the rush to resume.
Stray hairs white in my beard,
on my shirt, in slippers—marked.
Weather cool enough to open windows,
August in its grave. Welcome, Monday.
I sit trying to think about guilt,
aging. Trying again to fail again
and, as Beckett wagged, fail better.
Breezes deliver a whir of chainsaw
to my study, private production
of local melodrama *The Cedar Orchard*,
tale of priceless adjoining woods
raped for pennies. I struggle to
get hands around this redneck tragedy,
but Jasper won't listen. Collar jangle,
more heavy breathing, and there
the joyous beast stands, challenging
and immediate in my door. Between teeth,
braid of rawhide clamped obliquely,
authority of a canine Churchill
or Groucho in a fur coat. His birthday,
I recall, is Friday. 12 Big Ones.
He belly-flops, resumes furious gnawing
louder than the saw. Black eyes lift
and tongue lolls, as if to suggest
to a kind and obedient master: I'll wait
at your feet and enjoy my beefy
breakfast. When you wake from grousing,
rise from that blank machine, we can
tumble in grass and fall sunshine—
romp, circumstance, a play that matters.

Apologia on the Eve of Jasper's 12ᵗʰ Birthday

> To love that well which thou must leave ere long.

Week of grievance and posture.
Long week of revised goals,
diminished expectation. Week of boozy
bad sleep. In short, a flop of a week.
But tomorrow's my dog's 12ᵗʰ.
Neither of us, I believe,
quite recalls the minute detail
of how overnight he aged from five months
to twelve years, nor quite
the inspiration of our state-to-state exodus.
But his health for now is good,
he breathes easy, is white and beautiful.
For now, he's on the couch,
I'm on the floor, and we have
swallowed every morsel of our seared
foie gras and diced apple salad,
tongued each leaf of baby romaine
wilted in goose-fat/balsamic reduction,
and now, even as I speak, Jasper licks
the last Sauternes from the fountain of my palm,
last drops of the last
bottle from the Paris duty-free
—or was it Amsterdam?—
Barton & Guestier of Bordeaux, since 1725.
We, too, still remain, in our native
terroir, in our traditional manner.

Colophon

Bembo was modeled on typefaces cut by Francesco Griffo for Aldus Manutius' printing of De Aetna in 1495 in Venice, a book by classicist Pietro Bembo about his visit to Mount Etna. Griffo's design is considered one of the first of the old style typefaces, which include Garamond, that were used as staple text types in Europe for 200 years. Stanley Morison supervised the design of Bembo for the Monotype Corporation in 1929. Bembo is a fine text face because of its well-proportioned letterforms, functional serifs, and lack of peculiarities; the italic is modeled on the handwriting of the Renaissance scribe Giovanni Tagliente. Books and other texts set in Bembo can encompass a large variety of subjects and formats because of its quiet classical beauty and its high readability.

Cover Painting

Leonard Koscianski, "Under the Tree," oil on canvas, 46" x 66."

Thanks to Mr. Koscianski
and to Ethan Karp at the OK Harris Gallery, 383 West Broadway, New York.

Design by Robert B. Cumming, Jr.

GAYLORD BREWER is a professor at Middle Tennessee State University, where he founded and edits *Poems & Plays*. He has published 600 poems in journals and anthologies (including *Best American Poetry 2006*), six chapbooks of poetry, and five previous full-length collections: *Presently a Beast* (Coreopsis, 1996), *Devilfish* (Red Hen, 1999), *Four Nails* (Snail's Pace, 2001), *Barbaric Mercies* (Red Hen, 2003), and *Exit Pursued by a Bear* (Cherry Grove, 2004). His literary criticism includes *David Mamet and Film* (McFarland, 1993) and *Charles Bukowski* (Twayne/Macmillan, 1997), and his plays have been staged in Alaska, New York, Ohio, and Tennessee. Brewer's most recent residency was at the Obras Arts Centre in Portugal. He is a native of Louisville, Kentucky, and earned a Ph.D. from Ohio State University.

Printed in the United States
46831LVS00007B/466-549